MECCA

MECCA
The Muslim Pilgrimage

Photographs by Abdelaziz Frikha
Text by Ezzedine Guellouz

PADDINGTON
PRESS LTD
NEW YORK & LONDON

Library of Congress Cataloging in Publication Data

Guellouz, Ezzedine.
  Mecca, the Muslim pilgrimage.

  Translation of Pelerinage a la Mecque.
  1. Muslim pilgrims and pilgrimages—Saudi Arabia—
Mecca—Pictorial works.   I. Frikha, Abdelazis.   II. Title.
BP187.3.F73   297'.38   79-1125
ISBN 0 7092 0231 8 (pbk)
ISBN 0 7092 0232 6
US and Canada only:
  ISBN 0 448 22301 5 (pbk)
  ISBN 0 448 22302 3
Copyright © 1979 Sud Editions, 9 bis
rue de la Nouvelle Delhi, Tunis, Tunisia

The first edition of this book published by
Sud Editions, Tunis in 1977

Publisher: Moncef Guellaty
Coordinator: Ahmed Triki
Production: Abderrazak Khadhraoui and Leila Gasmi
Design: Hannelor Labidi
Filmset in England by SX Composing Ltd., Rayleigh, Essex
Printed and bound in Italy by pubbligraf

IN THE UNITED STATES
PADDINGTON PRESS
Distributed by
GROSSET & DUNLAP

IN THE UNITED KINGDOM
PADDINGTON PRESS

IN CANADA
Distributed by
RANDOM HOUSE OF CANADA LTD

IN SOUTHERN AFRICA
Distributed by
ERNEST STANTON (PUBLISHERS) (PTY) LTD

IN AUSTRALIA AND NEW ZEALAND
Distributed by
A. H. & A. W. REED

IN SOUTH EAST ASIA
Distributed by
FEDERAL PUBLICATIONS (Singapore)

IN INDIA
Distributed by
INDIA BOOK HOUSE

CONTENTS

FOREWORD

Each day a quarter of the world's population turn five times in prayer toward the city of Mecca, the spiritual home of Islam. They turn toward the Ka'bah—the first House of God built by Abraham and his son Ismael. This simple building stands in the center of Mecca's Sacred Mosque. It is the focal point for the prayers of a thousand million people throughout the world. For them it stands as the ultimate symbol of One God. The significance of Mecca is heightened by the fact that it was there that the Prophet Muhammad was born and there that he received his first revelation. It is to this holy city that millions of Muslims travel each year. They are fulfilling the command contained in the Koran that each person shall at least once in their lifetime make the pilgrimage to Mecca—the pilgrimage that is known to the Muslim world as the *Hajj*.

Year by year the number of people responding to this call increases. Muslims from the four corners of the earth, people of every race, age and background, come together to perform an extraordinary act of mass devotion. Inspite of their number and the diversity of the crowd, the atmosphere is always one of serenity and unity—over a million and a half people sharing the supreme moment of their lives.

The visual impact of this vast human gathering is unparalleled by any event in the world—it is an awe-inspiring spectacle that no non-Muslim will ever witness. Only now can they see it in photographs. Abdelaziz Frikha is one of the very first photographers to have been granted permission to cover the events of the *Hajj*. His photographs pay tribute not only to his technical brilliance but also to his sensitivity toward the people, his fellow pilgrims, with whom he lived and traveled throughout the pilgrimage in 1976 (1396 on the Muslim calendar).

To complement these outstanding photographs, a detailed, first hand account of the pilgrimage is provided by Ezzedine Guellouz, Chief Librarian of the National Library of Tunis. His experience on this, his first *Hajj*, proved to be a turning point in his life. His enlightening and moving personal diary unveils the complexities of the pilgrimage in simple terms but with deep insight based upon his broad knowledge of Islam. He explains the rituals, describes the day to day occurrences and problems of organization, and provides the historical and theological background to the events. Above all he reveals the deep significance of the journey both for himself and for the many pilgrims he came to know during his *Hajj*.

It is through Jeddah, Saudi Arabia's largest port, that most pilgrims arrive by air and sea from all parts of the globe. For days the new highway from the port to the city of Mecca is jammed with thousands of vehicles carrying the pilgrims. The Sacred Mosque, its minarets towering above Mecca, holds over half a million people but throughout the *Hajj* it is constantly overflowing with figures in white robes—the traditional dress of the pilgrim.

The Ka'bah stands in the center of the Mosque's huge courtyard, covered in the *Kiswah*—an enormous expanse of black cloth embroidered in gold with verses from the Koran. Embedded in the East Corner of the

Ka'bah is the Black Stone, placed there by Abraham. When Muhammad drove worshippers of pagan idols from the Ka'bah, restoring it as the Temple and House of God, he kissed the Black Stone. It is every pilgrim's desire to reach it and do the same before beginning the *tawaf*—seven circuits of the Ka'bah—a ritual which creates a human whirlpool around the sacred building.

The climax of the *Hajj* takes place ten miles from Mecca at Arafat on the barren plains of the desert. Here, on the Mount of Mercy, the Prophet Muhammad preached his last sermon. On this site the pilgrims come together for a day to form the largest gathering in one place, at one time and for one purpose that can be witnessed in the world today. Their one purpose is to stand in prayer "before God."

At dusk the pilgrims turn back toward Mecca and travel first to Muzdalifah where each pilgrim collects forty-nine stones. By the time they reach Mina, a tiny settlement a few miles from Mecca, the village has been transformed into an enormous tent city, erected to accommodate the pilgrims for three days and nights. In a symbolic rejection of evil, the pilgrims throw their stones at the huge pillars which stand in the center of Mina and represent Satan and other devils. The great Feast of Sacrifice which follows is celebrated simultaneously by Muslims throughout the world. This dramatic Feast, involving the sacrifice of animals, continues for several days as the pilgrims gradually make their way back to Mecca for the final rituals of the *Hajj*.

Although a visit to the beautiful city of Medina is not a religious obligation, few pilgrims can resist the opportunity of seeing its many sites of historical and spiritual significance. For it was in Medina that Muhammad created around him the first community of Muslims and it was there that he died. The magnificent Prophet's Mosque contains Muhammad's tomb and many pilgrims seek out the cool and peaceful interior of the Mosque in order to meditate and say their final prayers before returning to their homes.

Arafat and Mina now stand quiet once more in the empty wilderness of the desert. Mecca and Medina return to normal and hundreds of thousands of people board boats and planes in Jeddah. The pilgrimage to Mecca is at an end but the experience is carried home to the four corners of the earth to be shared with relatives and friends—an experience that will remain in the hearts of the pilgrims for the rest of their days.

And Abraham said: My Lord make safe this territory,
and preserve me and my sons from serving idols.
My Lord! they have led many of mankind astray
but who followeth me, he verily is of me . . .

KORAN XIV – 35

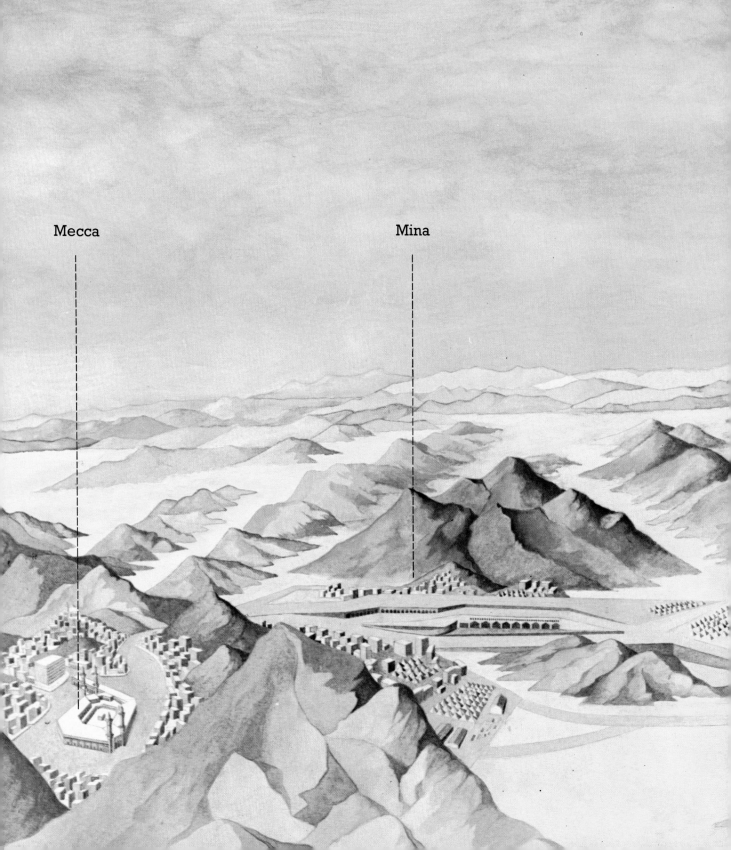

Mecca

Mina

THE HOLY PLACES

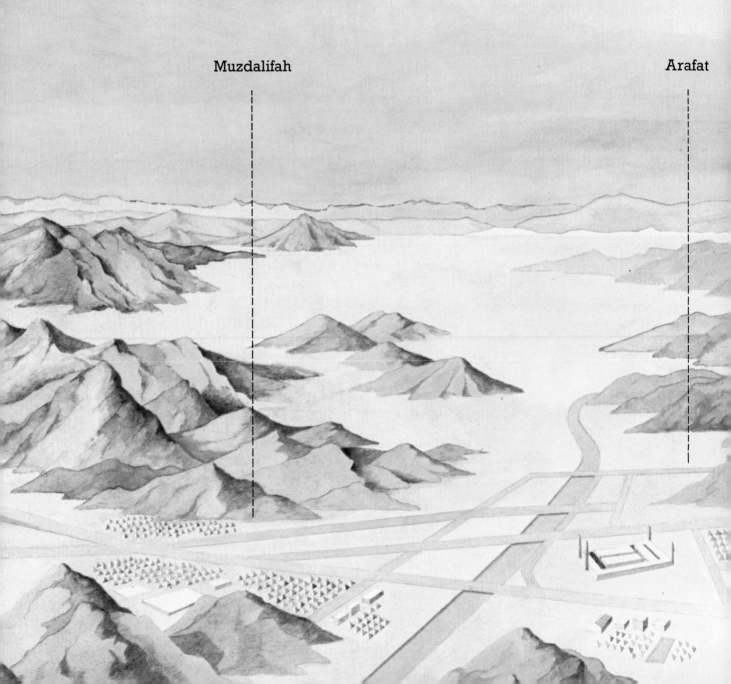

Muzdalifah

Arafat

And proclaim unto mankind the Pilgrimage. They will come unto thee on foot and on every lean camel; they will come from every deep ravine.

KORAN XXII – 27

JEDDAH

Jeddah, Saudi Arabia's largest port, receives millions of Muslims from all over the world. They arrive by air and sea to rest in the modern Pilgrim's Village before embarking on their journey to Mecca. The ancient town of Jeddah, with its narrow streets of intricately carved buildings, now stands side by side with a bustling modern city.

During the Hajj men adopt the distinctive clothing of the Ihram, two pieces of seamless white cloth. The Ihram refers both to the garment and to the rites which will be performed by the pilgrim. Women maintain their usual dress and their heads are covered at all times.

ey come from the four
rners of the world,
ople of every race and
lor, to hold a single
mmunion in worship of
lah and His Messenger

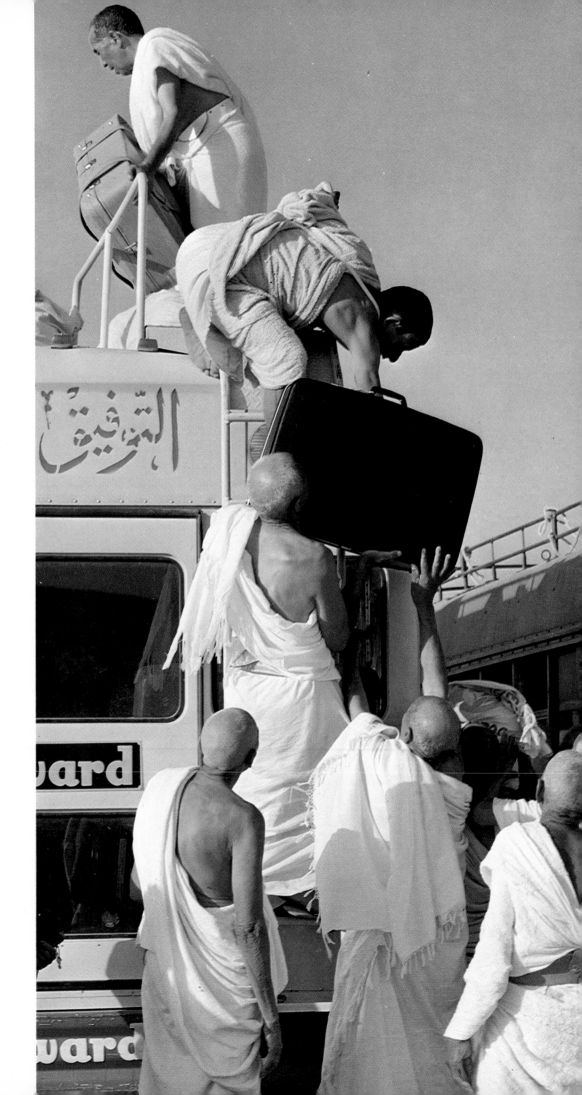

streetseller offers
ads to pilgrims as they
sten on their way.
any find places on the
vernment buses which
 continually from
ddah to Mecca.

*Lo! The first Sanctuary appointed for mankind was that at Mecca,
a blessed place, a guidance to the peoples . . .*
KORAN III – 96

MECCA

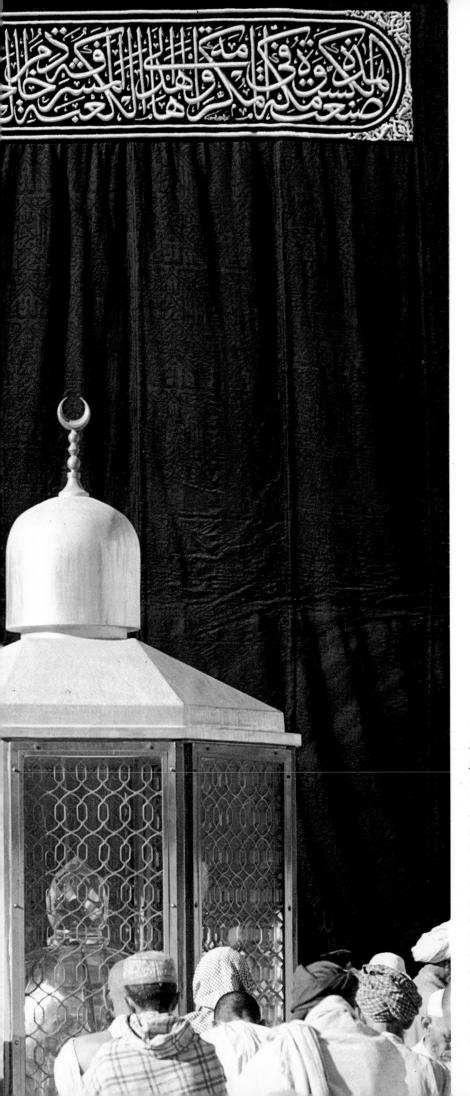

Throughout the world, Muslims turn to Mecca to pray. They turn to the Sacred Mosque and in its center, the Ka'bah. This ancient sanctuary, the first House of God, is draped in the Kiswah – a huge expanse of black cloth, embroidered in gold with verses from the Koran. Close by, in a gilded glass cage, is the stone on which Abraham stood in order to complete the building of the Ka'bah which he erected with his son, Ismael.

*A pilgrim prays to God
before the Ka'bah.*

The minarets of the Sacred Mosque tower above Mecca at night but below the city does not sleep – thousands of pilgrims continue to make their way toward the Ka'bah.

"I testify that there is no God but God and I testify that Muhammad is God's prophet...."

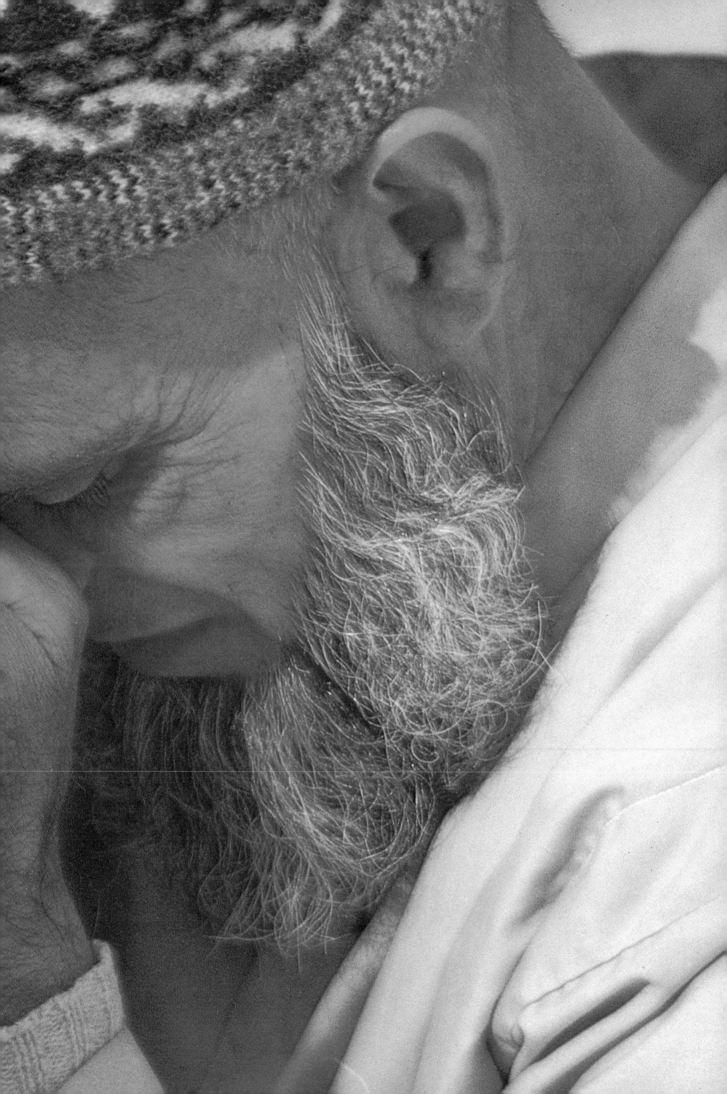

*Midday prayers in the
Sacred Mosque.*

e beautiful walkways,
ich lead from the
cred Mosque to run
tween the hills of
Safa and al-Marwa,
ntain another spectacle
ceaseless motion.
eir mosaic floors cover
e route taken by Hagar,
e wife of Abraham, in
r search for water. The
grims pass along the
ute seven times before
ding a quiet place to
lax, meditate or read
om the Koran.

*And hold fast, all of you together, to the faith of Allah,
and do not separate. And remember Allah's favor unto you:
how you were enemies and he made friendship between your hearts
so that you became as brothers by his grace . . .*

KORAN III – 103

ARAFAT

Arafat, situated on a barren plain ten miles from Mecca, is the setting for the next stage of the Hajj. Pilgrims flood into the spacious Mosque of Namira for midday prayer but only a small proportion can be received inside.

The setting sun signifies the hour of the maghrib prayer. Yet the pilgrims do not pray—instead they hasten away from Arafat, as did the Prophet, and head toward Muzdalifah.

Our Lord! Cause not our hearts to stray after thou hast guided us . . .

KORAN III – 8

MINA

Mina, a small and ancient town, plays host to millions of pilgrims for three days and nights. On their way from Arafat, each person has collected forty-nine pebbles in order to perform the ritual stoning of Satan, which takes the form of throwing the stones at symbolic pillars.

Vast walkways have been constructed to accommodate the pilgrims in Mina as they move toward the pillars. After the stoning of Satan, a symbolic rejection of evil, the pilgrims discard their Ihrams and adopt colorful clothes before the ceremonial slaughter of animals and the great Feast of Sacrifice.

*Anyone who performs the Hajj without visiting me
is being churlish.*

HADITH

MEDINA

A visit to Medina is not obligatory for pilgrims but most make the journey in order to visit the tomb of Muhammad in the awesome Prophet's Mosque.

One of the four towering minarets above the Prophet's Mosque in which a final prayer is performed near the site where Muhammed and his companions preached, prayed and lived.

The HAJJ

"Here am I, O God, at Thy Command, Here I am!"

JEDDAH

My neighbors in this bustling waiting room at Jeddah airport appear to me to come from Indonesia. Having noticed that I was looking in vain for a refreshment bar they offered me, in silence but with a warm smile, a soft drink.

"Thank you. Thank you very much indeed."

With the instinctive reaction of an old hand at international tourism, I spoke in English, as I have always done when meeting people from another part of the world. My neighbor smiled again.

"*Labbaika-Allahumma, Labbaik!* Are you British, Sir?"

"*Labbaika-Allahumma, Labbaik!* No, I am not British."

And, I tell him where I come from.

The land of my birth is thousands of miles from their native Djakarta or Bandung. And yet they are not in the least surprised to hear the "password" come quite naturally to my lips, as it does to theirs.

"*Labbaika-Allahumma, Labbaik!* (Here am I, O God, at Thy Command, Here I am!)"

Our "password" is this common response to the call, the words we repeat once we have entered the pilgrim's state of consecration: *Ihram.* With these words we scan every step, every incident, every occurrence on our march toward the rallying point, the march by which we are bringing to pass what God announced to His Prophet—that we would come "on foot or on the finest mounts from the farthest of the four corners of the earth."

The "finest mounts" in this year 1396 (1976) of the Hijrah (the Hijrah was the first year of the Islamic calendar) are the Boeings, Tridents, Tupolevs, Airbuses, and Caravelles that crowd the skies of Jeddah. For it takes countless aircraft to bring, in the space of two or three weeks, the huge number of pilgrims—more than half a million—in addition to the increasing number of other visitors to Jeddah. In other words, the airport copes with 50,000 travelers a day, about 2,000 an hour, or more than 340 a minute. This is the equivalent of three Caravelles every minute or two Boeing 747s every three minutes. And this supposes that the flow is continual, never stopping or slackening, night or day; a situation that I no longer find difficult to imagine now that I have seen for myself the reality of this human hive, for which no other mass gathering of people, anywhere else in the world, had prepared me.

Yet the 670,000 pilgrims arriving at Jeddah airport account for only a part of the total number of people responding to the call this year. Some 10,000 have landed at the airports of Medina, Dahran, Riyadh, Jizan and Najran. 90,000 have come to Jeddah by sea, and 3,000 have landed at the ports of Habar and Yanbu. 330,000 have passed through various border points on land. This year, well over a million foreigners will have visited Saudi Arabia in order to perform the *Hajj*, the annual pilgrimage. The Koran prescribes that every Muslim, provided he or she can afford it, should make the pilgrimage. It is one of the five pillars of Islam.

In 1347 (1927), when my grandfather, at the same age as I am today, arrived at Jeddah by sea, there were 90,764 foreigners; in 1382 (1962) my father, traveling by land, was one of 199,037 non-Saudi Arabians to come. The figure had doubled in those thirty-five years. In the past fifteen years it has quadrupled! How many will there be when my son, in his turn, sets off for the Holy Places?

Admittedly, when my grandfather and 90,000 other Muslims responded to the call in 1927, the total number of Muslims was 330,000,000, representing not more than 15 percent of the world's population. Today, as a result of massive conversions in many parts of the world, there are 1,000 million of us; that is over 20 percent of the world's total population. It should be noted too that the number of people who are able to perform the *Hajj* is also rapidly increasing. In 1929, less than fifty years ago, 0.027 percent of Muslims who were not natives of the Hejaz, (the western part of Saudi Arabia), made the pilgrimage—one Muslim in four thousand. In 1976, those who, at the same time as I, were preparing to perform the rites, accounted for 0.1 percent of non-Saudi Arabian Muslims: one Muslim in a thousand. The fact that the proportion has quadrupled is highly significant. Not only does it demonstrate the progress achieved in means of transportation, and the increased ability of Muslims throughout the world to afford these means of transport, but it is also a manifestation of the increase in religious observance in our community.

On the bus, conveying us from the runway to the arrival hall, we had been shown a row, at least five hundred yards long, of identical buildings. This was the *Madinat al-hujjaj* (the Pilgrims' City), one of the Saudi Arabian government's solutions to finding itself obliged to cope with an unprecedented influx of travelers. The Pilgrims' City is like a modern housing estate, consisting of buildings resembling the apartment blocks that one sees in the suburbs of any big city.

In the arrival hall, the pilgrims hand over their passports to a police officer, then identify their luggage and present it for customs inspection. The Saudi customs officers carry out their duties pleasantly, and neither the influx of pilgrims nor the accumulation of passports, however great the disorder may appear, disturbs their unruffled calm. Maintaining this outward appearance of calm is clearly the secret of their efficiency.

Once these formalities have been completed, the luggage can be entrusted to one's porter who loads it on to a trolley. These porters are supplied by the United Agency of *Mutawwifs* and are identified by a badge. The *mutawwifs* are literally "those who guide others on the *tawaf*"—the circling of the Ka'bah, a ritual performed at the Sacred Mosque in Mecca. They take charge of the pilgrims on the journey to Mecca and the Holy Places of Arafat, Muzdalifah and Mina. Formerly the *mutawwif* would meet the pilgrims on arrival in Jeddah. They made their presence known so that their clients could approach them. Most of them operated in the same way as a travel agent does, making preparations for the season, sending out leaflets to the area of the world from which they obtained their clients and sometimes touring the area themselves. For at least four generations, my family used the services of one family of *mutawwifs*. Each year when I was a child I had seen the representative of this family come and spend a few days with us in Tunisia in the course of his preseason tour.

This year I do not expect to see either our friends or their agents. The United Agency now has full responsibility for appointing *Hajjis* (pilgrims) to the individual *mutawwifs*. The porters, who belong to this Agency, are well-trained. They do not ask for immediate payment after carrying luggage to the Pilgrims' City, knowing that their clients have no means of paying cash at this stage. They provide useful information about Jeddah and point out the important places such as the banks and the Agency's offices. Then, far too suddenly for most pilgrims, the *mutawwifs* vanish, leaving their clients at the Pilgrims' Village to rest and wait, containing their souls in patience. In Jeddah one must be prepared to wait —with the enormous number of people involved, waiting is inevitable.

The pilgrims organize themselves into groups and then together they occupy the necessary number of rooms in the "apartment blocks." Like all buildings whose primary aim is to provide basic accommodation, the emphasis is on efficiency and economy rather than sophistication. Inside the buildings, there are no apartments as such but dozens of rooms, simply but adequately equipped with beds and bedding and served by communal washing and toilet facilities.

The younger and more active members of the group take the responsibility of going to the city center and making all the necessary arrangements for the *Hajj*. The first priority is to find the foreign exchange offices in order to cash the group's checks. Counters are marked with certain geographical zones to help the pilgrims. Money is required for personal needs and also to pay the entry dues for the *Hajj*. Today this payment is a token, since the Saudi Arabian government has taken over the financing of the *Hajj*.

The next stop is the Agency which assigns both *mutawwifs* and, where appropriate, *mutawwirs*—literally those "who conduct a visit," in this case the visit to Medina. A trip to Medina is in no way a rite or a religious obligation, but Medina is a beautiful ancient city of deep religious significance, so many pilgrims include a visit there as part of their itinerary for the *Hajj*. In both Mecca and the Holy Places, and in Medina, the pilgrims will stay in accommodation arranged by the Agency.

Handling so vast a gathering of human beings is a complex task for the authorities. There is no means of avoiding the fact that for about five days each year over 1.5 million pilgrims will converge on Mecca and the Holy Places. They will include those of us who are arriving at Jeddah, other foreigners who have already reached Mecca and are waiting for the *Hajj* to commence, and, of course, the Saudi Arabian pilgrims who number over 400,000.

Medina can avoid such a massive influx of people. Some pilgrims do not go there at all and, more important, they can make their visit either before or after visiting the Holy Places. With careful organization, the authorities try to ensure that half the pilgrims go at one time and half at another. The groups' representatives are informed by the Agency on which day they may enter the city. Pilgrims arriving early will begin their stay with the *ziyarah* (visit) to Medina, while others will go there immediately before they depart for home.

The other important arrangement to be made at the Agency is the means and time of transportation for the group to the Holy Places. The government assigns each group to a transport company and informs them of the times of arrival and departure from each town.

One cannot fail to be impressed by the efficiency of the Saudi Arabian government in organizing the *Hajj*. One aspect of the administration seems overwhelming and I cannot understand how it is coped with—that is finding the people who work specifically for the *Hajj*. The people who undertake the tasks of organizing this enormous number of pilgrims are often very young and work very long hours. I felt nothing but immense goodwill toward them as they performed their work seriously and efficiently but always with smiles and graciousness.

Not all pilgrims are subjected to waiting in the Pilgrims' Village for their representative to return with news of the arrangements that have been made. Official delegations are presented with a *bitaqat mujamala*, a courtesy certificate, which enables them to move between the towns without keeping to fixed dates. The main purpose of official delegations is to look after their country's pilgrims, and to convey to the Saudi Arabian authorities the messages of goodwill with which their governments have entrusted them.

There was a time when it was also one of their functions to deliver to the sovereign of the Hejaz the *Surra* (purse) containing a cash donation—their country's contribution to the upkeep of the Holy Places. Today, because of the advance in its economy, Saudi Arabia has absolved all other states from this commitment.

The monetary commitment to the Holy Places and the *Hajj* is no longer important but the spiritual commitment is still of enormous significance. Each year, every head of State of a Muslim country receives a delegation of pilgrims before they leave. He proffers advice and recalls memories of his own *Hajj* or other visits he has made to the Holy Places. Invariably he concludes by asking the prospective *Hajjis* to pay his respects to the Ka'bah—the Temple of God in Mecca—and to the Prophet's Tomb in Medina. Finally he asks to be remembered in their prayers.

My own Head of State asked me to perform a prayer for him and when he asked I would not have dreamed of protesting that I was unworthy. I was conscious of the importance of the mission he was asking me to undertake. It was a request I received from many, many people when they knew I was to make the pilgrimage—relatives, friends, mere aquaintances and, occasionally, complete strangers. Shopkeepers who guessed from my purchases that I was making the journey, invariably concluded each transaction with a request for a prayer. And I shall never forget the face of the stranger who, with tears in his eyes, watched me as the bus carried me toward my airplane for take-off. He was well aware that he did not know me and that I did not know him; that I could not hear him; but he was sure that I would understand his silent plea as he made a simple gesture toward me: he opened his hands, palms upward, before his breast. I understood.

Later I did pray for my unknown friend and for all the others who had asked me to do so.

The pilgrims' departure is a time of celebration. In my village it has always been marked by a simple but moving ceremony. The *mushayyin*, "those of whom leave is taken," which includes most of the people in the village, go to the home of each prospective pilgrim in turn. Hymns that have been handed down through the centuries are sung, their one theme being the *tashwik*, an invitation to nostalgia. They sing of the mystic beauty of the Holy Places, of the great happiness that one would experience if one were there and consequently one's burning desire to go there. Everything can and must be sacrificed to this ardent passion: love for one's birthplace, for one's family—everything. There will be tears for the *Hajji* is going away from his or her family, but the call cannot be denied.

Before I had boarded my plane I had entered the state of *Ihram*— dedicating my body and my soul to God. This is a serious commitment. Before leaving home I performed the *ghusl*, major ablution, and cut my hair and trimmed my nails for the last time, knowing that after entering the state of *Ihram* until the end of the *Hajj*, I must neither cut my hair or nails and that I must use no perfume. I know too that I must refrain from wearing not only headgear but also clothing of any kind, footwear included, which has seams. The only clothing allowed is two white sheets, one of which I shall wear wrapped around the lower portion of my body, and the other thrown loosely over one shoulder. The word *Ihram* is also used to describe this clothing. On my feet will be sandals made without stitching and I shall not carry any accessories other than a seamless belt to secure my wrapper and to hold money and papers. I know too that I must not take the life of any living thing, even the smallest earthworm or insect, and that I must refrain from sexual intercourse as long as my *Ihram* lasts.

Pilgrims enter the state of *Ihram* at varying stages of their journey to Mecca, depending where they are traveling from. The specific times and places are known as the *miqat* (assignment) of time and place. In my case the *miqat* of time and place was the moment our airplane was over Rabigh (a coastal town north of Jeddah). When I met my "brother" from Indonesia in the airport waiting room I could not guess his station in life for he was also in the state of *Ihram*—his clothing and footwear exactly the same as mine. I was aware that, like me, he would have in mind the *surahs* or verses from the Koran which I had recited when dedicating my soul to God on entering the state of *Ihram*. He would also be aware of the verses defining our common status.

The pilgrimage shall be made in the appointed months.
He that intends to perform it in those months must abstain from abuse,
lewdness and acrimonious disputes while on pilgrimage.

KORAN II – 197

Whenever discussions become heated, pilgrims will remind each other of these words. From the moment the pilgrims arrive in Saudi Arabia, inspite of the large numbers of people, the problems of organization and the inevitable waiting around, they remain serene and patient. This vast mass of people might, if it were not for their state of mind, easily degenerate into a jostling, unpleasant crowd. But the atmosphere of mutual respect excludes any possibility of this. Everyone who has experienced the *Hajj* will agree with me.

In Jeddah, the bustling activity in and around the Pilgrims' Village begins to give one an idea of what to expect during the *Hajj*, not only in terms of numbers and the surprisingly warm and polite attitude of all concerned, but also the enormous variety of people. One hears numerous languages and accents, and sees people of all races, all colors. I had plenty of time in Jeddah to wander in the busy lanes of the bazaars, purchasing any necessary items I had forgotten or had discovered damaged on the journey. However, I did not take advantage of this. Like me, most pilgrims take the time to see Jeddah on the return journey. It is a civilized city that, in places, teems with the activity of an ultramodern commercial center, in others bustles with a commotion that is apparently medieval in its colorful variety. But the *Hajji* has his sights on Mecca, he is like a magnetic needle that becomes feverishly agitated as it approaches the pole. The closer I got to Mecca, the greater my excitement.

After what seemed to be an extremely long wait, a police officer finally appeared in my group's quarters of the Pilgrims' Village, laden with hundreds of passports. He handed them around to their owners. The coach belonging to the transport company designated by the United Agency eventually arrived. As soon as we had boarded and loaded our luggage a call rang out from one voice—expressing the sentiments of all.

"Straight to Mecca, driver, and I will see that you receive a tip of one riyal from each passenger if we arrive in time for *fajr* (the dawn prayer)."

MECCA

Smile at your donkey or camel driver, keep on good terms with him throughout the journey, listen politely to his chatter—all these injunctions are part of the commandments that the perfect pilgrim obeys. Learned theologians emphasize these humble commonsense rules. For it is impossible to concentrate in complete serenity on a journey, each step of which is an act of devotion, if one is distracted by inefficiency or arguments with one's camel driver.

The 1976 equivalent of the camel drivers are the drivers of the thousands of cars, trucks and buses that unceasingly thread their way across the Hejaz at every hour of the day and night, covering the forty-five miles from Jeddah to Mecca. I realized how important it is not to add to the strain of bodies and minds that are already immeasurably overtaxed at this period of the year. "One hardly has time for one's duty to God," confided one of my fellow passengers. He meant that one hardly had time for the daily five prescribed prayers of worship.

We are on the road to Mecca. *"Labbaika-Allahumma* . . . Here are we, Lord, here are we. Here are we. Thou hast no peer . . ."

We must not allow the purpose and meaning of our quest to escape our thoughts by failing to make the response to the divine call.

Somewhere in the night there is a brief stop and our passports are collected and handed in at the "border post." It really is a border: no non-Muslim may cross it into the territory beyond. This is the reason for the pilgrimage visa issued by the Saudi Arabian authorities which differs from the visitor's visas for areas other than the Holy territory. The pilgrimage visa cannot be obtained from Saudi Arabian consulates in non-Muslim countries unless the applicant can prove that he or she is a member of the Muslim community.

A few miles farther on I hear someone saying, "We can now see the first houses of the outlying districts of Mecca." We all know what this means. Following the more experienced in our company, we repeat:

"Lord, grant that I may sojourn here and may the means of my sojourn be free of all suspicion."

There is nothing the *Hajji* fears more than jeopardizing the spiritual benefit of his pious journey by paying for it, or even for part of it, with funds acquired by unlawful or even questionable, means. This is why the *Hajji* takes care not to leave any unpaid bills behind him, that he allows his family and all those dependent on him enough to cover their needs and to provide against contingencies. He is even more scrupulous to insure that he makes no illicit profit during his stay in Mecca.

We hardly have time to repeat these words before we have covered a distance that must have taken our ancestors an hour to travel, and the moment has come to offer formal greetings to the City.

Lord, this holy land is Thy land, this city is Thy city and this man before Thee is Thy creature. I come toward Thee from a far country, burdened with many sins and with numerous misdeeds. Being in need of Thee, yet fearing Thy retribution, I implore Thee, of Thy great mercy, to receive me, to allow me to enter Thy Paradise, the garden of blessedness. Lord, as this holy place is protected by consecration, so protect my flesh and bones from the fire. Lord, spare me Thy chastisement on the day of Thy creatures' resurrection. . . .

My own words fill me with trepidation. I am straining to catch a glimpse through the coach windows of the streets of this city whose merits and privileges I identify with fear. But despite the many lighted doors and windows, it is difficult to distinguish them in the darkness of the night.

What is the significance of this ancient city to the millions who have traveled here? To understand it fully one must also understand the deep significance of the lives of Abraham and Muhammad. After rejecting the idols worshipped by his tribe, Abraham worshipped in turn a star, then the moon and the sun, but in each case only for a short time. When he found they could be eclipsed he ceased worshipping them and came to discover the True God. After his long quest he returned to the site where he had left his wife Hagar and their son Ismael. According to Islamic tradition, a wind arose and in the dust was revealed the outline of a temple. On this site Abraham, with the help of Ismael, built the first House of God. The city of Mecca grew up around that temple.

It was in this city that the Prophet Muhammad was born. In his time the temple was no longer the home of One God. Pagan idols were worshipped there. From the time of the Prophet's first revelation, he spent twenty years spreading the word of God, and gathering followers. In Mecca, the most wealthy of all Arabian cities, it was against the interests of the people of wealth to support Muhammad. He fought many battles against the enemies of Islam, and the most important was that at Mecca, when he drove the worshippers of pagan idols from the Ka'bah, the first House of God, and destroyed the idols. The Ka'bah was restored to its original function and God forbade anyone but Muslims from entering the sanctuary. And now, answering the call of Abraham and Muhammad, my companions and I have arrived to look upon that sanctuary and perform the rites of the *Hajj*.

Seeing a hundred or so bodies all dressed entirely in white and reciting words that I cannot catch, it is some time before I realize that they are in fact people who are dressed and behaving exactly as I am. Doubtless they are uttering words very similar to mine and proceeding, though in a group, each of his own accord, toward the same goal as me. The fact that all these people, myself included, are dressed uniformly, brings home to me my own responsibility as a *Hajji*.

Now my eyes are becoming accustomed to the night, and to this activity, so unusual for such a late hour. Here there is no frontier between night and day.

It has been clearly explained to us that immediately the *Hajjis* reach Mecca, they must go directly to the *Masjidul-Haram* (the Sacred Mosque) to greet the Ka'bah and perform the seven *shawts* (circuits) of the *tawaf al-qudum,* "the arrival circumambulation," the first three of which will be at a jogging pace *(ramal).*

This is what the Prophet did. In this manner he showed the believers of Mecca that he and his companions had not been weakened by the supposedly noxious air of Medina. Nor were they worn out by the trials of the *Hijrah* (exodus) or by the exile's existence into which they had been forced by the hostility of this very city to which they now returned as victors. But though they returned as victors, their primary ambition was to *run;* to give praise to the Eternal in His Temple.

We, the *Hajji,* do likewise. We allow ourselves only the time, in accordance with canonical provisions, to deposit our belongings in a safe place and to perform the *wudu* (minor ablution), for the *tawaf* is a prayer and like all prayer must be performed in a state of *taharah* (purity).

As soon as we have taken possession of our rooms in the very simple building allocated to us, which we share four to a room, we all meet at the bottom of the stairs, each secretly surprised to see his companions quite obviously as impatient as he. We are lucky that our group includes two professors of theology who have considerable experience of the *Hajj,* and we are keen to perform our *tawaf al-qudum* under their guidance.

Out in the street, we have only gone a few yards when suddenly there arises a call to prayer. Many times have I had heard that proclamation.

"God is most great. I testify that there is no other God but God. I testify that Muhammad is the Apostle of God."

But I would never have believed such a degree of melodic purity possible. Was it due to the technical superiority of the muezzins *(muadhdhin:* "he who calls to prayer"), or has the air of Mecca remarkable acoustic properties? I do not know the answer, but today, thirteen months later, I can still hear with delight those words rending the silky texture of the desert sky.

From everywhere there emerge thousands of white forms, including those of my companions. I am only slowly becoming accustomed to seeing myself as one of these white silhouettes. The road turns and rises. I look up and see before me, elegant and majestic, the profile of one of the minarets of the *Haram* or "holy place", in this case the Sacred Mosque. There are only two or three hundred yards to go—but what am I saying? I become aware now that everything around me is completely stationary and has been for a moment or so; and then I realize that all the cars, trucks and buses are not parked there for the night, as I had supposed, but have just this minute stopped to allow their passengers to alight. Having done so, they now stand shoulder to shoulder with the mass of pedestrians.

The pedestrians are hardly moving either, for despite the fact that the Sacred Mosque has room for 500,000, it is already full. For hundreds of yards around it is surrounded; there are thousands of people behind me, although I had thought I was at the back of the crowd. The faithful are preparing to pray, under the guidance of an *imam* whose voice they can hear through the thousands of unseen loudspeakers that cover the city.

The only prescription governing the validity of this prayer is that there should be no gap in the ranks of the faithful, and from what I can see, I know that there is no gap, not even the smallest.

A worshipper beside me points to the ground with a commanding gesture: he has spread out a small square of cloth and is inviting me to share it with him for the prayer that has just begun. I must remember henceforth always to have with me my little prayer mat if I want to be ready to pray at all times and without too much damage to my forehead and kneecaps. I find I am deeply imbued with a feeling of solidarity with this man, whose few days, or perhaps only a few hours, longer stay in Mecca have given him authority over me, an authority which he silently exercises, and in a simple but practical manner that cements our brotherhood.

This discovery dominates my *ruku* (bowing) and my *sajda* (prostration). The phrases which I follow coming from the fine voice of the distant *imam* (preacher) today take on new significance for me, stemming from the realization that I am uttering them at the same time as this man who has made a point of sharing a cloth with me. This feeling is heightened by my certainty that from the *imam* to me there is an unbroken chain, formed entirely of links each as strongly joined as we are, my unknown Muslim brother and I.

Let nothing divide you, says the Lord; remember the favors He has bestowed upon you; how He united your hearts when you were enemies so that you are now brothers through His grace; and how He delivered you from the abyss of fire when you were on the very brink of it.

To be delivered from the fire: this is our hope, and one that can be fulfilled for we have just been given the certainty that our faith will be strengthened. It is also our hope because, standing here together, we have proof that our hearts are united.

The meditations of the Koran with which we shall accompany every step of our journey fill us with wonder as we discover their living meaning —their validity for the people and situations that Muhammad encountered in his daily life fourteen centuries ago and, at the same time, the validity of their teaching and the relevance of their message today.

Our eyes see, our feet tread, our hands and our foreheads touch this soil which our senses tell us is no different from any other. We understand, through direct contact with the physical and human realities to which the Word refers, those concrete truths that were formerly abstract notions: faith, brotherhood, salvation.

The *salam* (salutation denoting the end of prayers) is barely finished, when the *imam's* voice invites us to join in the *salat al-janaza* (funeral prayer). It should have occurred to me before that in a gathering of 1,500,000 there cannot be fewer than 150 deaths a day, so on average there will be 30 deaths to remember at each ritual prayer. During each prayer we shall recall our fellowship with the dead which, far from causing one to forget

101

one's fellowship with the living, fortifies it because it makes us aware of their frailty and our own. It also emphasizes the strength of the bonds uniting us.

Already engines are humming, and the cars, buses and trucks are beginning to move. Prayers are over and our little group is reunited.

A *Hajji* should enter the Sacred Mosque for the first time by the *Bab as-Salam* (the Door of Salvation).

"Lord, Thou art Salvation and from Thee alone comes Salvation. We beg Thee therefore to receive us, grant us Thy Salvation, and admit us to Paradise, where Salvation is to be found."

Who is speaking? Are the words I hear coming from my own lips, or are they being spoken by my unknown neighbor, by the thousands of strangers around me, my brothers?

I do not have time to decide whether I myself have pronounced the ritual words or whether they have been spoken for me. The portal under which we were passing is already behind us. Beyond it, if I am correct, is the inner courtyard of the Mosque. It is still dark, and being completely taken up by my invocations and by the spectacle of the crowd, I had seen little beyond the portal itself. But having passed it, I become aware that our progress is slowing down. We stand still. I raise my eyes.

I see now the simple cube draped in black cloth, somewhat faded by a year's exposure to the hot sun of the Hejaz, as it melts into the dimness of the dawn. It appears almost unreal, as if it were suspended rather than standing on the ground. The worshippers that move around it in a trance look as if they are the plinth of the Ka'bah, bearing it aloft in triumph.

I find tears flowing down my cheeks. I am no longer the same man that I was a few moments ago. I am no longer the disbelieving or indifferent person I have been at times; I am no longer the abstract believer that I was. I was over anxious to understand and to analyze, both others and myself; to put myself, my every gesture, in perspective. Perhaps, at the back of my mind, was the idea that I would later need to find the right words to describe all this, to explain it to intellectuals like myself. I no longer know that philosopher that I was. I no longer recognize him in myself.

No, I am now merely a man with tears running down his face. Fortunately, the words that I am required to recite are simple, saying precisely the things that I want to cry out at this moment.

"God is great! God is great! There is no other God but God!"

And my tears continue to flow. I say my prayer with my face bathed in tears. I feel as if I have been bathed within, flooded within.

My companions signal to me to join them. The time has come to launch ourselves into the teeming mass of bodies. There are so many people and it is impossible to imagine that a moment may come when the crowd will be less dense. Linking arms, we cling to each other firmly, forming a square, with the less strong, in particular the women, in the middle. Admitted to the *Hajj* on exactly the same terms as men, the women perform all the rites and are subject to the same conditions as men except as regards clothing. They do not don the pilgrim's garments but dress as usual. Although the *salah* (ritual prayer) is not obligatory, and is not even permitted to women when they are indisposed, the Law does not consider it fair that they should be forbidden participation in the *Hajj*, the most noble of all acts of faith. The Prophet said to Aisha, his wife, when she claimed on behalf of her sisters the right and the honor to fight beside their menfolk, "But to perform the *Hajj* is an exacting combat."

And indeed it is exacting; it is impossible to convey any idea of the effort required to perform, in the period of the *Hajj*, the seven circuits of the Ka'bah that form the circumambulation. It is impossible for the tens of thousands of people there to take any initiative at all. The motion of the human whirlpool seems to be independent of the will of those who are part of it. Yet each of us knows what to do. First, we begin each of the seven circuits by greeting the East Corner, known as the Black Stone Corner, a greeting which may, when this is possible, consist of kissing the Black Stone, but may equally well take the form of a simple gesture of greeting toward the Stone. There is of course no mention of the Stone in the ritual prayers so that no ambiguity is possible. It is to God that our prayers are addressed, not to the Stone. Umar, the second Caliph, proclaimed this aloud, saying.

"I know you are nothing but a stone, that you have no power to do either good or evil, and if I had not seen the Prophet greet you, I would not do so."

And one's gesture of greeting may be accompanied only by the words: "In the name of God; God is most great, God alone we praise, Glory be to God!"

Then one follows the wall of the Ka'bah, keeping it on one's left and staying as close to it as possible. In actual fact, one is moving alongside the base, the *sadhirwan*, and one passes, not in front of the Door of the Ka'bah, but below it. Here one sees the faithful struggling to climb up to touch the door, and a policeman has had to be posted there, in order to restrain the more adventurous. Between the Black Stone corner and the door there is a part of the wall, or more precisely of the base, called *Multazam*. This means "that to which one is attached" in both senses of the word: for it is here that the faithful, following the example of the Prophet, try to "attach" themselves to the Ka'bah in an embrace; they also recite the prayers that form a pact, a commitment to God. They jostle each other to be able to say, on this spot, a ritual prayer. But there are also many other less formal demonstrations of piety. I saw an old Bedouin woman dancing in front of the Ka'bah. But I was not tempted to laugh, or even smile at the sight. It is impossible not to be moved at the sight of any demonstration of faith, however rough or clumsy. I remember too the words that a twelfth-century traveler heard in the same place, being addressed to God by a woman of the Zayla tribe of Yemen, a people who then had a reputation of being particularly primitive: "Lord, You know that I am not as clever at praying as all these people, and You well know that I want from You just the same as they hope for, so grant me exactly what You grant them." I think also of another peasant whom the same writer reports as saying: "Lord, all these people have chosen what they want to ask of You, I ask You to choose for me."

The people around me are no less gifted for moving and simple prayers. Here there are no longer any differences of intellect among the thousands of faithful addressing their prayers around the Ka'bah to the One and Only God. This is no leveling down but a general appreciation of the symbolic significance of the most humble gestures and words.

We must go round the *Hatim*, the semicircular piece of wall that surrounds the northern parvis or enclosure of the Ka'bah. We must avoid stepping over into the parvis, which is called the *Hijr Ismail* (Ismael's precinct). This area was actually part of the original temple and as the circumambulation consists in making a circuit *around* the Temple, to step into the *Hijr* has the effect of canceling the circuit. One passes the corners of the Ka'bah known as *Rukn Shami* (Syrian corner) and *Rukn Iraqi* (Iraqi corner), on either side of the *Hatim*, without greeting them, but one must greet the *Rukn Yamani* (Yemen corner), the fourth and last, before beginning another circuit.

Learned believers have composed special invocations for each stage of each circuit. Although very moving, these invocations are in no way obligatory, no more than are those recited on arriving at the outskirts of Mecca, or upon entering the *Haram;* everyone is free to invoke the Lord of the Ka'bah in his own manner. The value of these texts is to list the multitude of prayers that a soul overflowing with faith, gratitude, veneration and hope can wish to formulate. On the other hand, it is obligatory to make seven circuits, and to leave the circling mass of bodies at the Black Stone corner at the end of the seventh circuit.

From there one goes to *Maqam Ibrahim* (Abraham's station), to offer a prayer. The faithful who are performing their *tawaf* leave little space, so once again we link arms in a protective barrier around the one who is praying, and each takes a turn to pray.

One feels unburdened, certainly, but exhausted too after such a test and when the *Zamzami* (bearers of water from the Zamzam well) appear we all rush toward them. It is not obligatory to drink the water of Zamzam, but in imitation of the Prophet we do so anyway, in great quantities. Later, before leaving, we shall fill flasks and water bottles with it, or take little sealed bottles of the water known as *Zamzamiya*. There is no present that relatives and friends will appreciate more than a bottle of the water of Zamzam, for it is "efficacious for whatever reason it is drunk."

There then follows the *sa'y*, the walk between the hills of al-Safa and al-Marwa: this consists of covering the distance, 460 yards, partly at a jog, seven times. Here, the Saudi Arabian architects have overcome the problems of the crush. An air-conditioned walkway *(masa)*, paved with marble, provides two one-way passages for those performing the walk, and also, in the middle, two others, one in each direction, for wheelchairs carrying people for whom the exhausting 1.5-mile walk is physically impossible.

Above the ground floor there is another level, laid out in the same way.

At the exit of the *masa* one of my companions, a professor of nuclear physics, said to me, trying to make it sound as casual as possible: "One feels better, doesn't one?" Yes, indeed one does feel better! Since experiencing such happiness on seeing the Ka'bah for the first time and being bathed in tears, I have been asking myself the reasons for this radical transformation that I have undergone.

I cannot take my eyes off the Ka'bah whenever we are within sight of it, or keep my thoughts off it when I cannot see it.

I try analyzing, or rather I begin to examine, this historical paradox, the conversion of a former Arab pantheon where 360 idols were worshipped into a temple of the most intransigent monotheism: the first House of God, One God. Deep within myself I find the answer. The ardor of the idolaters who were Muhammad's contemporaries was only human. Within people there lurk pressures, motivated by intellectual and spiritual laziness, that are only waiting for an opportunity to seize power within us and to replace the most hard-won convictions by superstitions. It is not just the worship of *al-Lata*, *al Uzza*, *Habal*, *Asaf* or *Naila*, the deities of the *al-jahiliyah* (the period of pre-Islamic Arabia) or in the West Jupiter, Apollo, Minerva and Mercury, that turns man from God. More perfidious is the adulation of money, power, fame and ambition.

Worship at the Ka'bah teaches that Islam, the religion of Truth and Realism, does not deny the existence and the permanence of these passionate aspirations. What Islam does assert is that such aspirations are evidence of man's thirst, of his quest for a life beyond himself. As such they are respectable. But as soon as such longings become an end in themselves and what they stand for is forgotten, it turns into idolatry and distracts Man from himself and from the One and Only God who made him in His image. The cult of the Ka'bah is considered by some to be taken from pagan rites. In fact it has been regained, taken over from paganism, by Islam and restored to its true sense—the worship of a Single God, in the way that was laid down by Abraham. For that prophet who destroyed idols, and built the Ka'bah, House of the One and Only God, was above all the prophet of the religion of *firra*, (simplicity). Simplicity is perhaps the most precious of qualities but also the quality most severely threatened by the forces that set man at war with himself. The true meaning of the word *islam* (so often ignored) is literally "surrender." It means surrender in the sense that the Muslim yields to a call—the simple call of common sense, both native and divine, within himself; the call that draws him upward and which he decides to obey. This call is obeyed at the cost of denying many of the passions and instincts that drag him downward.

The Ka'bah's simplicity of form, its beauty that is unsurpassable precisely because it is so simple, the simplicity of the spontaneous actions performed around the Ka'bah to express the worshippers' homage to God, all address themselves to native common sense, so constantly threatened yet ever present, and exert an appeal that will be forever real.

ARAFAT

Arafat stands in a natural amphitheater, about two and a half square miles in area. Here, on the Mount of Mercy, the Prophet Muhammad preached his last sermon. Each pilgrim must spend some time, however little, standing in this area on a particular day, before the sun rises to greet the new day. This is the Standing at Arafat, an essential part of the *Hajj*. If it is not achieved, then all the other rites and all the effort the pilgrim has made are nullified. To not reach Arafat by the assigned time is a nightmare which haunts all pilgrims.

Admittedly, I did not see this unhappy occurrence and it must happen very rarely these days with the provision of modern transport. Nevertheless theologians have provided for this eventuality. If a pilgrim comes within sight of this Holy Place at the very last moment, as the dawn is about to drive away the night ordained for this Station, it is sufficient to throw an object into the amphitheater so that it will reach Arafat in time. This accommodation for latecomers indicates the extreme importance that each one of the million and a half pilgrims attaches to not "missing." The verb "to miss" in some Muslim countries actually contains the meaning "to miss the Arafat Station."

Keeping this fact in mind, the state of mind of the drivers who take over a hundred thousand vehicles packed with pilgrims from Mecca to Arafat can be imagined.

Nothing, not even the crowd at Mecca in the preceding few days, could give any idea of what we would experience on the road to Arafat. Traffic jams cannot be prevented, even with the dozen or so highways that have been constructed or are in the course of construction between Mecca, Mina and Arafat. Despite all appeals to remain calm and cool, my companions are growing excited. The threat of "missing" becomes particularly agonizing as we near our goal, so much so that our driver, though a very courteous and very calm man, yields to the repeated requests of his passengers. As it is impossible to move forward on our highway because of the congestion, and as the various unfinished highways are not separated from each other by fences or by deep ditches, our driver decides to take a risk. He asks us to get out and then, with his heavy vehicle, leaves the road and tries to cut across country to join the neighboring highway. The wheels miss the track and the coach is stuck—unable to move either forward or back.

Our anguish lasts about three quarters of an hour. We pray that a police helicopter has noticed the awkward position of our vehicle, or that our predicament has appeared on the screen of one of the closed circuit televisions. Eventually a police truck equipped with towing gear arrives and another coach is asked to help with our rescue. I have the impression that our driver is not being congratulated for his initiative. But the people of the Hejaz rarely raise their voices, even in an argument. It is more unlikely that they would do so on a day of *Hajj* when, despite the many precautions, the most advanced equipment, and the almost unlimited investments made, problems still occur.

The impact of this enormous gathering cannot be over-emphasized. The coming together of men and women, regardless of sex, nationality race, or social condition, is the very object of this ritual. The believer, who at last manages to find a spot somewhere in the immense canvas city that Arafat is transformed into, finds it striking but not strange, to see how literally the Koranic and the Prophetic word fits situations that were undreamt of when the Word became known.

For the Prophet, reconquering Mecca and converting to Islam the places of the *Hajj*, first involved the subjugation of the leading clans of the Quraysh, Muhammad's own Meccan tribe. While not wishing to humiliate them or indulge in pointless revenge, Muhammad insisted that they be brought down to the level of ordinary citizens of the great City of God with no privilege either through birth or fortune. In Mecca it was precisely in religious affairs, specifically in the administration of the Ka'bah, and the pilgrimage, that the privileges of caste had become so evident. The Qurayshites considered the Temple as their own preserve, and imposed their authority, sometimes very harshly, on others using the Temple. For example, the special clothing required for the circumambulation of the Ka'bah could be obtained only from the *Hums* (Quraysh and Qurayshite clans). Consequently, anyone to whom the *Hums* refused this clothing was obliged, if he wanted at all costs to perform the rite, to do so naked. Likewise, the Qurayshites insisted on their privilege of performing their *ifadah* (the "onrush" toward the valley of Mina which follows the standing at Arafat), not from Arafat, as the commoners did, but from Muzdalifah, thus not having to leave the sacred territory of Mecca.

These and other privileges were expressly declared impious by the Koran; Muhammad, although himself a Qurayshite, demonstrated the Koran's insistence on equality by staying with the mass of the people at Arafat.

At Arafat, during his *Hajj al-Wada* (Farewell Pilgrimage), the Prophet, in his last sermon, stressed the importance that Islam attaches to the principle of equality—equality without social distinction; equality that implied the sharing of rights and duties by husband and wife. In the same address he referred to the supremacy of the law and its corollary: the injunction against taking the law into one's own hands. He also stressed the prohibition of usury, without which the assertion of equality before the law would be meaningless. And it is particularly significant that the Prophet's last message should link this assertion of equality between people to the performance of the pilgrimage rites. How impressive it is that a message prompted by, and applicable to, the Prophet's own time should be equally applicable to our life fourteen centuries later.

This brotherly communion is the keynote of the Station at Arafat. A city of tents, with geometrically straight streets and avenues, has been pitched the day before. This is the one day when the services of the *mutawwif* (guide and courier) will be essential and when he will be most appreciated. He will have been allocated one or more plots of land where he sets up his tents and the sanitary and cooking facilities that enable his "clients" to pass the day without too much practical inconvenience. A client who gets lost among all these "streets" and "avenues" (named only by numbers, as they are in New York) can be brought back to his point of departure if he gives his *mutawwif's* name.

The *Hajji*, on this day, has thoughts only for God. Although in normal circumstances it is possible to make up for prayers after their appointed hour, this is not recommended on the day at Arafat. On the other hand, as he is traveling, the *Hajji* is entitled to shorten his prayers and to say them together, two by two. Customarily, the shortened prayers of *dhuhr* (noon) and *asr* (midafternoon) are said together. They are celebrated in this form at the enormous Namirah Mosque, situated at the entrance to Arafat, where they are preceded by a sermon delivered by the *Amir al-Hajj* (the leader of the Pilgrimage), to commemorate the Prophet's sermon when he performed his *Hajj al-Wada*. Generally speaking, the Station at Arafat starts after these prayers, but in point of fact one is free to perform it according to the dictates of one's conscience.

Specific verses of the Koran are recommended for reading while one stands in the amphitheater. Also, many prayers have been composed for the occasion. Neither the verses of the Koran nor the prayers are obligatory—one must express one's devotion to God in one's own way.

In the immense plain, overlooked by the majestic mountain range of the *Ta'if*, one can witness almost as many different attitudes and gestures as there are people. Alone or in groups, sitting or standing, motionless or walking about, on foot or seated in their vehicles (as in former times our ancestors were authorized to remain perched on their horses or their camels), each in his own way invokes the All-Powerful before whom they have the good fortune to come today.

From our camp, I can see the Jabal ar-Rahmah (the Mount of Mercy), a small hill from which the Prophet gave his last sermon. Between 90,000 and 100,000 people accompanied him on the Farewell Pilgrimage. I am told that there will be a series of speakers and preachers there today, but I do not want to join the crowd listening to them. To truly understand my brothers, with whom I want to enter into communion, I feel I must experience some quiet reading and meditation. It is only by fully understanding myself that I shall be able to understand others. As if to strengthen me in my urge for meditation, silence seems to be spreading throughout the tens of thousands of people whom I had found too noisy for my liking a short while ago.

Facing toward Mecca, but without having to make any ritual gestures, everyone lowers their voice. A few yards away from me, I catch sight of a face bathed in tears and twisted with sorrow: it is an intellectual who I came across on the first day at Mecca. Then he was declaring that he did not even know the lines of the *Ikhlas* (twenty words in all) and he told me he had come on the pilgrimage just "to do his duty."

The setting sun finds us in our various attitudes of devotion. It is the hour of the *maghrib* prayer. And yet we do not pray now. Instead we strike camp, as did the Prophet. This is the *ifadah*, or "onrush." As quickly as possible, we race away from Arafat. Our "finest mounts" are at the ready. That is to say that motors are being started and drivers are calling those of their passengers for whom they are still waiting. It is just as if we had suddenly remembered an important appointment to attend elsewhere, a meeting which could not be postponed.

The first effect of this rush is to strengthen our "communion." After our prayer and meditation as one, which has just made us irrevocably *Hajjis*, our departure with every person hastening away together emphasizes the significance of our gathering in this place.

Our bus, like all the others, is moving forward at a crawling pace. Only a few years ago, it took some *Hajjis* twenty-four hours to travel the few miles between Arafat and Muzdalifah, our next stage. Yet everyone is relaxed. We were in a hurry because the rite lays down that we should leave Arafat rapidly and together, but we are no longer anxious; the other rites that we still have to accomplish do not have to be done in haste.

Conversations begin. As far as I can remember, the discussions were solely about points of doctrine or religious practice. When does performing the *asr* (or *dhuhr* or *isha*) prayer cease to be "normal observance" and become "restitution?" Is it true that it is preferable to wait until as late as possible in the night after *isha* to perform prayers beyond those required by God? Another subject of conversation which fascinates those around me, and which I too find interesting because it is quite new to me, is the times of the day not to perform the *nafila* (voluntary) prayers.

I am surprised to be feeling this curiosity and passionate interest in religious inquiries. Previously such discussions have always seemed unnecessary concern with detail, and an excuse for pointless argument.

Emerging "cleansed" from our Station at Arafat, we are all preparing to lead, from now on, a life actively committed to God. We are full of good resolutions. It is not at all surprising, therefore, that we should want to know, for example, the hours that canonical law decrees should "not be devoted to prayer." Each of us is convinced that from today we will find nothing more urgent to do than to meditate and pray.

Eventually our coach arrives at Muzdalifah. In the dark of night, and especially because of the headlights that sweep the horizon, I am unable to discern anything of our surroundings. In particular, I am curious to know how far we are from *Mashar al-Haram* (the Sacred Monument), which I had caught sight of some time before when it was still daylight.

We are here to perform a rite specifically laid down by the Koran. Immediately after the *ifadah*, that is after the faithful have "hastened forth" from Arafat, everyone is required individually to "remember God by the Sacred Monument," to remember God as He who has guided the people along the straight path, when they had gone astray. The "straight path" starts from Arafat. Arafat is not the last point of a spiritual journey, but the starting point of a New Life, the birth of a New Man.

We are aware that the place where we now stand was once dedicated to the pagan god *Quzah*, the god of tempest and storm, from whose name comes *qaws quzah*, "Quzah's bow," the Arabic word for rainbow. Such places as this where pagan worship took place have since been transformed by Islam into places of adoration for the One and Only God. Here we stop to remember God, the Koran states, "As ye remember your fathers, or with a more lively remembrance."

We are aware that the Prophet's prayers and his worthiness have made it possible for us at last to benefit from God's mercy. It is said that it was at Arafat that Muhammad obtained remission for all our sins; all except the "injustice that we have perpetrated against one another." The Prophet learned that God would give redress to those who had been sinned against, and that therefore all sinners could be pardoned. At Muzdalifah, "the place where one makes oneself agreeable," the New Man takes time to appreciate the immensity of his heavenly bliss now that he has been cleansed of all sin. In view of this happiness, he considers that it would be very petty to continue to harbor bitterness toward anyone who has sinned against him and he learns to show compassion to all. The supreme gift that God made to the Prophet at Muzdalifah was to dispel all resentment and bitterness from our hearts.

Each of us, conscious that he has sinned as much as, or more, than he has been sinned against, sets great store by this divine gift of reconciliation with our neighbors. It is only by forgiving others that we can be at peace with ourselves.

The rites at Muzdalifah begin with prayer, the last two prayers of the day—*maghrib* (sunset) and *isha* (nightfall). This time I have to prostrate myself on the bare ground, not having had time to pick up my little prayer mat. I can feel the small pebbles digging into my kneecaps and my forehead.

Prayers have barely finished when I see my companions dispersing, looking closely at the ground, each busy collecting with great care about seventy pebbles. Later, in the coach, they will carefully sort these, keeping only forty-nine of more or less "standard" size—no smaller than a chickpea, no larger than a lima bean.

These stones will come into use the next day. For tomorrow and the following days at Mina, a few miles away, the faithful will symbolically demonstrate their determination to resist the temptations that they know will continue to waylay them all along their painful path of life. It is important that these stones should be collected here and now, for use in the rite which, repeated methodically and insistently, denotes the pilgrims' rebuttal of all temptations to yield to weakness. For the same symbolic reasons, it is important that the preparatory measures for the resistance that is to last an entire lifetime, should be made immediately after the two stations, at Arafat and Muzdalifah, in the course of which God's pardon and that of humanity have been obtained.

Unburdened and cleansed, armed with shining new faith and hope, I would like to be able to follow the Prophet's course and sleep in this place. But in this day and age, it is not necessary to rest here.

However, I lie down on my right side for one minute, just long enough to recite the invocations with which I customarily prepare for sleep. Then I rejoin the coach.

MINA

The unavoidably slow progress of our coach gives us plenty of time to gaze at the steep escarpments rising on either side of the road which run from Muzdalifah to Mina, or rather from Arafat to Mecca passing through Muzdalifah and Mina. For the whole route is one and the same mountain pass, broadening out a little at Muzdalifah and more noticeably at Mina.

Such a confined space could not contain the "onrush" which every year becomes more spectacular. Consequently sections of the mountains have had to be sliced away to make it possible to build the dozen or so highways that enable today's *Hajjis* to follow as closely as they can the road the Prophet took for his Farewell Pilgrimage. Admittedly, for us there is no possibility, either going or coming back, of choosing between the various routes or of taking for the return journey a different road from that of the outward journey, as the Prophet did. With all the goodwill of the Saudi Arabian government, and however great its financial contribution, one does wonder how, from the technical point of view, it is ever going to be possible to find room for further development.

Despite the darkness, we can distinguish our surroundings fairly well, for on every square yard of the mountainside there are lights from tents, shacks and other temporary structures. The density of people settling on the ground increases the closer one gets to Mina, and the more the valley widens. Eventually one can see the luminous structure of the *al-Khayf* Mosque, the largest in Mina. And to the right sprawls the biggest camp-site I, or anyone else, will ever see.

Hajjis stay here for at least three nights and three days (known as the days of *tashriq*). Consequently, there are many shops and services in addition to the tents. Normally there can be no more than a few hundred inhabitants in Mina, a village with only two streets, but during the days of *tashriq*, this tiny settlement has to accommodate more than two million people. The authorities certainly do their best to insure that there is some degree of order, but, for several reasons, it is more difficult to control the flow of people here than it is at Arafat.

Firstly, the duration of the pilgrims' stay in Mina is longer. Also, it seems to me that the religious tension that imbues the life of the *Hajji* from the moment of his arrival until he reaches Arafat wears off at Mina. Here, not everyone is a *Hajji*, and the *Hajjis* themselves are no longer as devout as they were in Mecca and Arafat, where they were concerned only with the perfect performance of a rite and the strict purity of their attitude and thoughts during the accomplishment of that rite.

In fact, of all the rites of the *Hajj*, those performed at Mina are the most difficult to understand and to explain; their symbolic significance is the least easy to understand for the uninitiated and their fundamental meaning is therefore more frequently twisted than is that of the other rites. They are significant, however, and this significance is no less rich than the significance of each of the other rites.

The forty-nine pebbles carefully gathered and sorted at Muzdalifah are to be thrown, in accordance with a very meticulous ceremonial method, at three baetyls (sacred pillars) set up at intervals along a distance of 300 yards running across the Mina site.

These baetyls are called *Jimar* or *Jamarat*, which means "stone" or "landmark" and is used both for the pebbles that are thrown and for the pillars at which they are thrown. The one nearest to Mecca is called either *Jamarat al-Aqabah*, after the name of the place where it is situated, or *al Jamarat al-Kubra* (the Great Jamara). The second, 130 yards farther on, is known as *al Jamarat al-Wusta* (the medium or Middle Jamara), and the third, 170 yards on, at the Muzdalifah end, is called *al Jamarat al-Ula* (the First) or *al-Sugra* (the Small Jamara). On the first day at Mina seven pebbles are thrown at the Great Jamara alone, and during the following two days seven pebbles are thrown at each of the three, beginning each time with the Small Jamara.

If one respects the spirit and the letter of the Tradition, each of the forty-nine throws is accompanied only by the words: "God is great. There is no other God but God. Our praises are for God alone." This is all that is prescribed and all that is permitted, in imitation of what the Prophet did. In the Koran there is no reference to this rite.

Regrettably, most of our fellow pilgrims do not display much restraint in their words and gestures, as is evident from the mere sight and sound of the incredible throng as it invades the area. The Saudi Arabian authorities have devised a sensible scheme for the route. An overpass has been built above the road, which it follows exactly. It has three "hollows" out of which rise the baetyls and into which the pebbles fall. One can throw them either from the road or from the overpass. The pilgrims are supposed to take the road in one direction and the overpass for the return. But unlike the walk between the hills of al-Safa and al-Marwa in Mecca, where the one-way traffic flow works perfectly, here people do not respect the recommended routes despite constant reminders on signboards in both Arabic and Roman script.

There is an atmosphere of indescribable excitement attached to this rite. For although theologians refrain from calling the ritual anything other than *ramyol-jimar*, the "throwing of the pebbles," in the vernacular of all Muslim countries, including the Hejaz region itself, it is referred to as *rajm as-shaytan*, the "stoning of Satan." The *Jamarat* themselves are known in some countries and provinces as *Iblis* and in others as *Shaytan Akbar*, *Awsat* and *Asgar* (Great, Medium and Small *Iblis* or Satan). Popular legends, describing the rite, invite the faithful to stone *Iblis*, Satan himself, and also mention lesser devils. This explains the violence with which people throw their stones. Apart from cases of people being hit on the head by stray pebbles, I also saw, falling into the hollows, stones whose size was nothing like the stipulated chickpea or lima bean. I saw hundreds of sandals piling up at the foot of the baetyls, thrown by those for whom seven pebbles were apparently insufficient to express their hatred of the enemy.

The words that one hears people saying or shrieking, needless to say bear no resemblance to the calm invocations to the Omnipotent that are prescribed by the Tradition. The expressions on the faces range from strain to torture. My initial reaction was to protest against such excesses, which pervert the rite and divorce it from its original meaning. I even said as much to those nearby. But, all things considered, such subversion is understandable. These men and women believe that they should manifest their antagonism toward the newly discovered source of their past errors and faults. In their own way, they are demonstrating how they intend from now on to make a complete break with the forces of evil. And that includes such "evils" as laziness or cunning. No one wants to jeopardize the conversion gained by their experiences at Mecca and Arafat.

The connection of the baetyls to Satan stems from a popular legend not authenticated by any text. It is believed that the baetyls of Mina mark the path followed by Abraham and his son Ismael, and perhaps his wife Hagar, when they were going to the place where the Lord, to test Abraham's devotion, had asked him to sacrifice his son. The baetyls are said to mark the three places where Satan appeared to Abraham and his family in an attempt to dissuade them from obeying the divine command. Neither does orthodox Tradition corroborate the site of the *madbah* ("the place of immolation") where Abraham was about to plunge his knife into his son's throat. It is said that on this site the *kabsh* (ram) appeared in time to redeem Ismael when at last the faith and obedience of both father and son had been sufficiently established in God's eyes.

Mina is also the location for another major ritual of the *Hajj*—the Feast of Sacrifice, a dramatic celebration. Each pilgrim makes the sacrifice of an animal—usually a sheep, goat or camel—and part of the meat is cooked and eaten at Mina. The rest, traditionally, is given to the poor. As well as offering thanks to God, the *hajjis* are showing their readiness to give up their worldly possessions and to share with those who are less fortunate than themselves.

Today, the quantity sacrificed is far greater than the amount the local needy are prepared to take away. In an age of food shortages in many parts of the world, people question this slaughtering of animals, most of the carcasses having to be destroyed as rapidly as possible to avoid stench and disease. It is a problem that has concerned not only the Saudi Arabian government but also the religious authorities and other Muslim countries for several decades now.

The full performance of the rites of the *Hajj* demand that animals are sacrificed—giving alms of equal value is not permissable. In the year of my pilgrimage, 1396 (1976), nearly one and a half million animals were slaughtered. The authorities ensure that there is no risk of disease and plans are being made to find a solution to the problem of wasting the food.

I endeavored to spend the days of *tashriq* as prescribed by doctrine. I began by throwing my seven pebbles at the *Jamarat al-Aqabah*, and then traveled the short distance to Mecca to perform the *tawaf al-ifadah*. This is a circumambulation of the Ka'bah following the "onrush" from Arafat. It is an obligatory rite, unlike the circumambulation on arrival. This time I did not follow the encircling of the Ka'bah with the walk between the hills of al-Safa and al-Marwa; the walk that one performs upon arrival is the only one required, and indeed the only one permitted, in the course of any one *Hajj*.

Thereafter, I was able to cut three hairs from my head and to remove my *Ihram* garments. This symbolized my return to "ordinary" life, except with regard to sexual relations which were still forbidden until the end of the period assigned for sacrifices. Then I returned to Mina for two consecutive days, where I methodically threw seven pebbles at each of the three baetyls. As I could not recollect having committed any fundamental offence during my *Hajj*, I did not have to make any sacrifice, which spared me a visit to the spectacular abattoirs.

So here I was, a full citizen of Mecca. I was exultant. I was at last free to contemplate the Ka'bah. Making more *tawafs*, I tried at every hour of the day and night to touch the Black Stone, and hoped I might even, at long last, be able to kiss it. For various reasons, my stay in Mecca was limited to a mere two days.

Firstly, I had to spend a few hours on performing an *Umrah*, a "lesser" pilgrimage, which like the *Hajj* itself, is an obligation. My companions and I once again don our *Ihram* garments. The first free taxi driver we find, seeing us dressed in *Ihram* clothing after the days of *tashriq*, asks, "*Umrah?*" We do not have to tell him where we wish to go. He knows that he has to take us outside the boundaries of the sacred territory of Mecca, for we are required to enter the city anew.

At *At-Tanim*, the nearest border point, stands the Mosque of *Aisha*. We find it besieged by other prospective *Umrah* pilgrims who consider it meritorious to begin their "lesser" pilgrimage with a prayer in this mosque named after the Prophet's wife. With less formality we settle, as did *Aisha* herself, for a prayer in the open air. Then we get back into our taxi, and once again find ourselves repeating, "*Labbaika-Allahumma, Labbaik.*" A few minutes later we are back at Mecca, whose outlying houses we greet with the same phrases as we used a few days before for the *Hajj*. Our taxi deposits us near the Sacred Mosque where we make our circumambulation followed by prayers at the *Maqam Ibrahim* and then the walk between al-Safa and al-Marwa. Before leaving, we allow a barber to clip three hairs from each of us, and then we can resume the ordinary life and dress that, on this occasion, has been deprived us for only two hours.

Between the time of the *tawaf* that I performed as part of this *Umrah*, right up to the *tawaf al-wada* (the farewell circumambulation), and during the many visits I made both at prescribed prayer times and at other times, I had ample opportunity to contemplate the Ka'bah. The simple act of gazing at the Ka'bah is an act of devotion and a devotion that cost me nothing; from any angle, at whatever hour of the day or night, the sight of the Ka'bah always enraptured me. I never tired of contemplating a structure whose sole visible feature is its extreme simplicity. I realized that simplicity is the least imperfect expression of perfection, just as the unsurpassable

117

taste of pure fresh water outclasses the most sophisticated liqueurs.

Unfortunately, unlike dozens of other *Hajjis* whom I met, I was never able to reach the Black Stone myself. Some of my companions said that they had succeeded in doing so only when they made a *tawaf* at 2:00 PM in the afternoon, during the extreme heat, or at 2:00 AM in the morning, when it was very cold. Even so, despite following their advice and instructions, I failed, whether I tried in the very early morning or in the heat of the afternoon, or at any other time for that matter. At all hours I found the same dense whirlpool of people, preventing me from making a way through to the Stone.

Recently, when I was recalling these memories, and my regrets, with an older *Hajji*, he gave me this advice:

"Let yourself be carried along; do not seek a path for yourself."

Whether or not his words were intentionally symbolic, I shall endeavor to remember them on the occasion of my next *Hajj* or *Umrah*. When taking leave of the Ka'bah, at the foot of the Multazam, I did, in fact, beg God that this encounter with His Temple should not be my last.

I have quite recently learned that some theologians advise against using the common expression *"tawaf al-wada"* (farewell *tawaf*) and advocate that it should rather be called *"tawaf as-sadr"* (the departure *tawaf*), a name closer to my own feelings on my leaving Mecca. *I was not returning from Mecca, but merely setting out.*

MEDINA

"Anyone who performs the *Hajj* without visiting me is being churlish."

These words are those of the Prophet. I cannot imagine any pilgrim who would dream of being churlish toward the Man who received and gave us God's Message, the infinite richness of which becomes increasingly evident with each step of the way on our *Hajj*. Every one of us is consumed with the desire to express our gratitude and respect to the Man who was entrusted by God with the immense and fearful responsibility of conveying the Word to us.

The *Hajj*, amongst other things, prompts us to remember how concerned the Messenger of God was to be equal to his mission. Recently, when rereading the sermon on the occasion of the Farewell Pilgrimage, I was reminded of a moving expression of this desire. The Prophet had just given his last words of advice:

"All Muslims are brothers. No one may take what belongs to his brother, unless the latter has freely given him permission to do so. Take good care therefore not to do one another injustice."

Muhammad then called out, "O Lord, have I truly proclaimed Thy message?"

The crowd of faithful responded, "Lord, he has proclaimed Thy commands."

Again the Messenger appealed to his Creator, "O Lord, be my witness today."

Muhammad, a man of the people, had the feelings of any human being. Yet, because of his especially keen awareness and sensitivity, he particularly feared and apprehended God's judgment of his life and work. Such fear and concern are in keeping with the love that he bore for the community whom he urged to hear the call of truth. He always declared, without fear of offending his companions and his family, that this community that he loved so deeply would include all those who, living in other times and places after him, would receive the Message.

When asked by some of his companions, "Who could be more dear to you than we, your companions, O Messenger of God?," he replied, "Those who, coming after my time, recognize me without having known me."

It is precisely because Muhammad makes no claim to divinity that this chain of love between him and us must not be broken. So we go to Medina in order that we may in our turn bear witness that he has conveyed God's message, and add our prayers to those of countless generations of Muslims who have begged God to bless His last messenger and to reward him according to his merits. On our turn we will be the messengers for our family and friends who have asked us to convey their greetings and their blessings to Muhammad ibn 'Abdillah.

For the most illustrious Meccan is not buried at Mecca. At the age of fifty-three he was obliged to leave his home town to seek refuge some three hundred miles to the north, at Yathrib, which subsequently took the

120

name of *Madinat ar-Rasul* (City of the Prophet) and which is often referred to as *al-Madinah-l Munawwara* (the Enlightened City), or more commonly Medina (the City).

So attached were the Meccans to their prejudices and their privileges, that thirteen years of preaching peace had still not convinced them of the advantage of acknowledging the lucid message brought by their fellow citizen, although he was respected for his truthfulness and his honesty. In fact, they called him *al-Amin* (the man of integrity). Neither were they impressed by the fact that the equality that he preached and the abolition of idols that he called for, went against the interests of his own caste, the civil and religious aristocracy of the town, and even against his interests as an individual. At a certain point they ceased to contest the validity of Muhammad's tenets; all that worried them was the threat his teaching held for their vested interests.

Knowing that his life was in danger, Muhammad was forced to flee. His enemies had conceived a plan, perfectly suited to the social structure of Mecca, whereby he would be stabbed simultaneously by men belonging to all the clans of the town. Muhammad's own clan could not then demand vengeance, being unable to name one assassin and therefore one clan to prosecute. Another reason for leaving Mecca as soon as possible was the fact that a great number of the middle class of Yathrib (later to be known as Medina) had, for some time, been expressing their interest in the new religion. Many had been converted and had sworn allegiance to Muhammad. The *Hijrah* (Exodus) from Mecca to Medina was such an important turning point in history that the Muslim era, including its calendar, dates from it.

During their stay in Mecca, few *Hajjis* consider visiting the places connected with various periods in the life of the Prophet. For a start, they wish to avoid anything that might sooner or later degenerate into idolatry. The probable place of the Prophet's birth is not pointed out to visitors. One can pass in front of the Municipal Library of Mecca without suspecting that it stands on that supposed spot. Likewise, only a few think of visiting the cemetery of *al-Ma'lat* where Khadija, Muhammad's first wife, is buried, or even the house nearby where the Prophet lived. There are more visitors to the Jabal an-Nur (Mountain of Light), the sight of the Ghar Hira. This is where Muhammad used to withdraw to meditate before the revelation, and where he, an illiterate, found he had been chosen by God to "read," and give the world a Book. One can also visit the Ghar Thawr (the Cave of the Bull), where Muhammad first took shelter with Abu Bakr, one of his disciples, when God instructed him to leave Mecca.

It can be said that nothing has been done by the people of Mecca to promote the historical associations of their city's sites.

Mecca remains the City of Transcendence.

One gets a totally different impression of Medina as you enter this beautiful city. Custom is partly responsible for this. At Medina there is no question, as there was at Mecca, of rushing straight to the Mosque upon arrival. It is recommended that one should first of all get settled in, and wash and dress as a normal tourist.

In Medina one is the Prophet's guest; dress and behavior should naturally show the great deference and deep love felt for him, but anything that might be confused with worshipping him is avoided.

A walk around the town confirms this impression. The city has been very carefully planned, and it is both efficient and elegant. The main streets near our hotel impress me by the number of shops and by the abundance, quality and good taste of the goods on display. There are watches and clocks, jewelry, radio and television appliances, and further on, textiles and clothing, leatherwork and travel goods. Because of the low rate of taxation and import duty in Saudi Arabia, the prices of many foreign goods are lower than in their country of origin. In particular, gold, radios and televisions are very popular purchases with visitors.

Medina has more to offer than jewelry or electrical goods. In the Suq as-Saha and Suq al-Manakha there is an atmosphere like that of the bazaar at Istanbul or the souks of Tunis and Fez. The friendly shopkeepers welcome you, offer coffee and cigarettes, and patiently help you accumulate a pile of presents for your family and friends. No gifts brought home from other journeys give their recipients as much pleasure as those from the Holy Places. Nobody must be left out. In contrast to the customary, often excessive, Islamic reserve when it comes to accepting gifts, relatives and friends never refuse a present offered by a *Hajji* on the occasion of his or her return. Furthermore, they sometimes even demand one. This should be considered an honor, for it demonstrates the veneration felt for the Places from which one has come and of which one is now considered to be part.

On every one of my shopping expeditions held, naturally, between prayer times, I accumulated dozens of strings of prayer beads. They are made in Hong Kong, and formerly in Birmingham, England. I also purchased minute editions of the Koran that I had seen being made in Czechoslovakia, and tins engraved to depict Mecca or Medina.

However, I brought home more than just souvenirs. A few of my friends would receive wall hangings, the works of a silk calligrapher whom I was very pleased to find, and I ransacked bookstalls and bookshops.

I also indulged a passion, which goes back to my early childhood, for Medina dates, with their wonderful hint of caramel. Until then, I had only had one or two of these dates a year.

My taxi driver was full of praise for the customs and character of the people of Medina and I had to agree with him. As the name of their exquisite city suggests, their foremost quality is their charm. But it seems that their politeness is not just good manners, it goes much deeper, stemming from kindness and generosity. The Koran refers to the people of Medina: "They love those who have emigrated to their town and give them first choice, even when they themselves are in need." Times have changed, of course, and we, the emigrés of today, are not exactly in need. But at Medina I was invited into a citizen's home, and I do not think I was the only *Hajji* to be shown such hospitality. From the hotel keepers, the restaurant owners, shopkeepers, and every one else I came across, I met with nothing but friendliness, and it was friendliness without servility.

In this warm atmosphere I visited many of the famous sites of Medina. At places where important followers of Muhammad and members of his family are buried, there are always large gatherings of people. Notices warn that it is forbidden to prostrate oneself by the tombs. Policemen are posted nearby to ensure that this rule is obeyed. Excessive demonstrations of piety at such places are regarded as idolatrous—people are to be respected not worshipped.

On the road into the city, just outside Medina, is an elegant Mosque built on the site where the very first Mosque was built by the Prophet and his followers. He had been given a *mirbad* (an area for drying dates) and it was here that the Mosque was constructed.

Another important Mosque, that of the Two Qiblas, shows traces of the fact that in very early days the followers of Islam prayed toward Jerusalem. According to some, it was on this spot that it was revealed to the Prophet that he should change the direction for Mecca. At the time he was half way through saying *dhuhr*, or noon prayers, and changed direction to complete them facing toward Mecca.

The main reason we have "saddled our mounts" and traveled to Medina is to visit *Habibna* (our friend) Muhammad. So the most significant visit of the stay there is to the Prophet's Mosque.

The building is magnificent, adorned with intricate stone carvings and beautiful mosaics—it has been added to over the centuries so the craftmanship of many generations is displayed here. After entering by the magnificent gateway we follow the recommended itinery, reciting the words we have been advised to repeat: "In the name of God the Merciful and Compassionate; from God alone comes all strength and power. God bless our Lord Muhammad, Thy servant and Thy Prophet . . ."

As we make our way into the center of the building, we come near to the *minbar*, a place of great spiritual significance since the Tradition tells us that the Prophet was accustomed to praying in this exact spot. The crowd here is large and my companions and I protect each other while we perform our prayers in turn.

Then we make our way to the room which contains the Prophet's tomb. Our greeting is simple: "Peace be upon you, O Prophet, and the mercy and blessings of God!" It is nothing more than one might say for a friend. No voice is raised, no one bows or makes any gesture toward the tomb, and it is forbidden to attempt to kiss the structure. All books of religious instruction stress the importance of abiding by these sanctions. One prays to God to bless Muhammad and to reward him for what he did in the service of God and for the salvation of humanity. We also convey to the Prophet the greetings of those who begged us to carry them.

Taking one or two steps to the right of the tomb, one is level with the head of Abu Bakr—the first Caliph and Muhammad's closest friend. His tomb is parallel with the Prophet's but set back, so that the Caliph's head is level with the feet of the Messenger of God. One more step to the right and one is level with Umar's head, the second Caliph. His tomb is set even further back from that of his illustrious predecessor. To each we address a greeting in accordance with our knowledge of their lives.

For a few moments, the tears flow from my eyes once more. They are gentle tears, like those we shed when we meet those we love. I have a feeling of trust and warmth, of closeness with those I respect most. We would like to spend several hours in this serene and inspiring building. It is said that one should spend enough time at Medina to perform the "prescribed forty prayers" which in fact take a whole week. Although this is what we would most like to do, we do not have the time.

In the short time we did have, I visited the Prophet's Mosque as often as possible. At the times of the prescribed prayers the Mosque is crowded so I wanted to go there long in advance of the hour of prayer in order to find a place to meditate and read. Obviously this was not the time of year to even attempt such a thing. I did see one incredible sight—a *Hajji* who recited here the whole of the Koran from the first to the last verse. He did it all from memory.

The extensions and decorations of the Mosque have transformed it from the original modest oratory that stood on this site. But present-day visitors should not be distracted by the architectural splendor from meditating on the simple truths this place represents—here, in a small, modest enclosure Muhammad preached, prayed and lived.

I was lucky enough to be present for Friday prayers in the Prophet's Mosque. The *imam* who preached there stepped aside to the Prophet's tomb to request permission to preach from His pulpit before ascending the steps. This moving tradition is, of course, peculiar to Medina, but it recalls the legend that applies to all Muslim pulpits. The Prophet's first pulpit was an ordinary block of tamarisk in which three steps had been roughly hewn. When the Prophet died, Abu Bakr, out of respect for his predecessor, preached from the second step. After Abu Bakr's death, Umar preached from the third step.

Later, Marwan, Governor of Medina, raised the plain block on to a base of six steps. Today, standing on the seventh step, the Prophet's successors maintain a distance between themselves and the Messenger, in respect of his memory. What is most important and significant about this simple tradition is the fact of His presence on the pulpit, at the top of the steps.

The empty steps are symbolic of every Muslims' aspiration—to keep their place in the chain of knowledge that goes back to Muhammad himself and to keep alive the Message given to the Prophet by the One and Only God.

The Islamic World Map

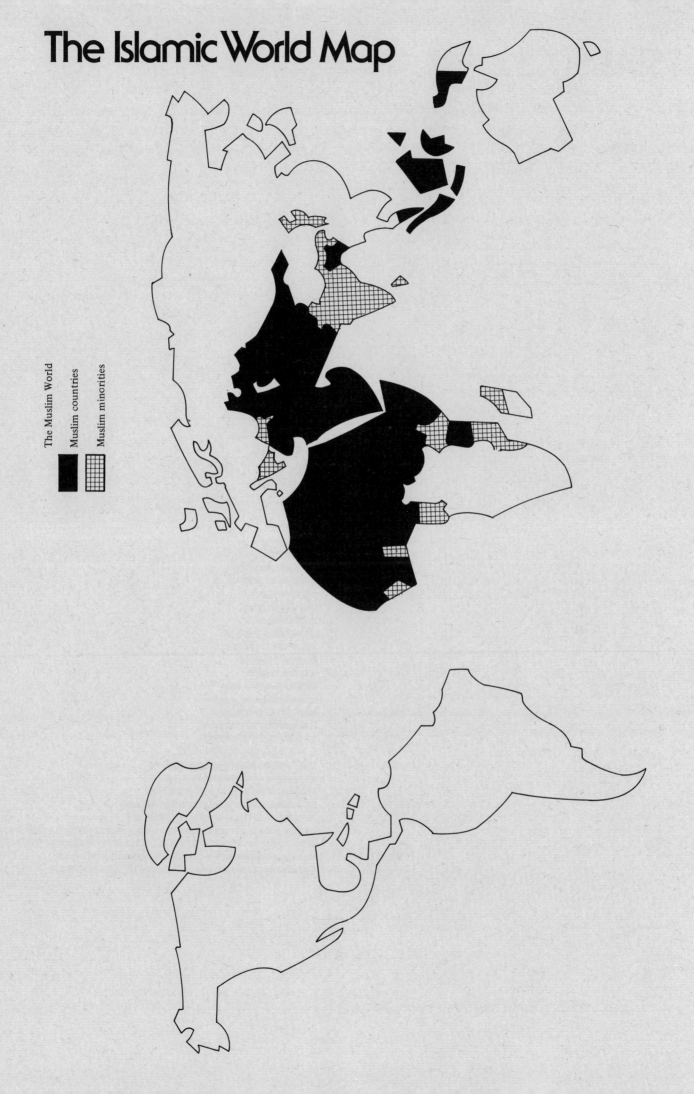

The Muslim World

Muslim countries

Muslim minorities

STATISTICS

Total number of pilgrims in 1977   1627 589

Non-Saudi pilgrims

Saudi nationals from Mecca
178.360

Saudi nationals from the rest of the country
213 769

Non-Saudi residents
496 141

Non-resident foreigners
739 319

Total annual entries, 1927 to 1977

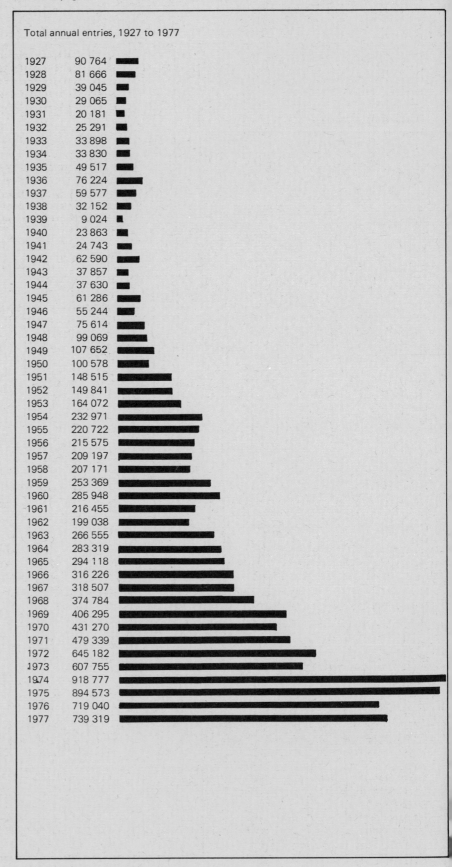

1927	90 764
1928	81 666
1929	39 045
1930	29 065
1931	20 181
1932	25 291
1933	33 898
1934	33 830
1935	49 517
1936	76 224
1937	59 577
1938	32 152
1939	9 024
1940	23 863
1941	24 743
1942	62 590
1943	37 857
1944	37 630
1945	61 286
1946	55 244
1947	75 614
1948	99 069
1949	107 652
1950	100 578
1951	148 515
1952	149 841
1953	164 072
1954	232 971
1955	220 722
1956	215 575
1957	209 197
1958	207 171
1959	253 369
1960	285 948
1961	216 455
1962	199 038
1963	266 555
1964	283 319
1965	294 118
1966	316 226
1967	318 507
1968	374 784
1969	406 295
1970	431 270
1971	479 339
1972	645 182
1973	607 755
1974	918 777
1975	894 573
1976	719 040
1977	739 319

Non-Saudi pilgrims, in 1977, by country of origin

Afghanistan	6,590
Algeria	53,230
Bahrain	2,269
Bangladesh	5,815
Benin	205
Brunei	201
Cameroon	990
Central African Empire	621
Chad	1,720
Djibouti	590
Egypt	30,951
Ethiopia	1,121
France	642
Gambia	99
Ghana	2,982
Greece	197
Guinea	1,244
India	21,113
Indonesia	35,703
Iran	36,942
Iraq	34,909
Ivory Coast	1,129
Jordan	14,211
Kenya	590
Kuwait	3,187
Lebanon	3,815
Liberia	80
Libya	20,770
Malaysia	4,278
Mali	2,740
Mauritania	1,084
Mauritius	315
Morocco	22,674
Niger	2,854
Nigeria	104,577
Oman	2,429
Pakistan	47,591
Palestine	1,434
Philippines	784
Qatar	1,139
Senegal	4,825
Sierra Leone	20
Singapore	731
Somalia	4,786
South Africa	765
Spain	52
Sri Lanka	407
Sudan	32,353
Syrian Arab Republic	24,829
Tanzania	1,086
Thailand	233
Tunisia	7,914
Turkey	91,497
Uganda	4,621
United Arab Emirates	3,560
United Kingdom	1,309
Upper Volta	1,995
Yemen, Democratic Rep.	7,599
Yemen Arab Republic	79,347
Yugoslavia	1,115
American countries	473
Other countries	2,661

Pilgrims

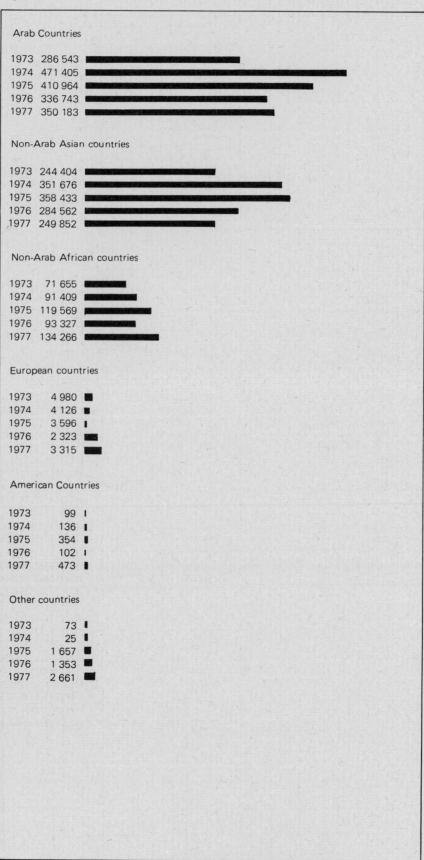

Arab Countries

1973   286 543
1974   471 405
1975   410 964
1976   336 743
1977   350 183

Non-Arab Asian countries

1973   244 404
1974   351 676
1975   358 433
1976   284 562
1977   249 852

Non-Arab African countries

1973   71 655
1974   91 409
1975   119 569
1976   93 327
1977   134 266

European countries

1973   4 980
1974   4 126
1975   3 596
1976   2 323
1977   3 315

American Countries

1973   99
1974   136
1975   354
1976   102
1977   473

Other countries

1973   73
1974   25
1975   1 657
1976   1 353
1977   2 661